THE NEW ASTROLOGY

Libra

BY
SUZANNE WHITE

Copyright © 2018 Suzanne White
All rights reserved.

The New Astrology
Libra

A Unique Synthesis of the World's Two Greatest
Astrological Systems: Chinese and Western
By
SUZANNE WHITE

The New Astrology
Suzanne White

World rights Copyright ©1986-2018 Suzanne White

Copyright notice: *This work intended it be solely for the buyer's personal use and enjoyment. Please do not re-sell, copy or give this product away. It has been officially registered with the US copyright office and, as such, is protected by law. If you would like to share my work with others, by all means feel free to purchase an additional copy for each of them. If you're reading this chapter and believe that my copyright has been violated or think it may be a pirated copy that was not paid for, please write to me: suzannwhite@aol.com to inform me of the violation in order that I might take steps to remedy the situation. I have at my disposal: hexes, spells and other metaphysical tools specifically designed to encourage readers (and pirates) to honor and protect my copyright. SuzanneWhite © 2012-2018*

TABLE OF CONTENTS

WHAT IS THE NEW ASTROLOGY? 5

WHY DOES THE NEW ASTROLOGY WORK? 5

WHAT IS THIS BOOK ABOUT? 6

LIBRA 6

THE CHINESE CALENDAR 9

LIBRA ~ RAT 18

LIBRA ~ OX 22

LIBRA ~ TIGER 26

LIBRA ~ CAT / RABBIT 30

LIBRA ~ DRAGON 34

LIBRA ~ SNAKE 37

LIBRA ~ HORSE 41

LIBRA ~ GOAT 45

LIBRA ~ MONKEY 49

LIBRA ~ ROOSTER 53

LIBRA ~ DOG 57

LIBRA ~ PIG 61

OTHER BOOKS BY SUZANNE WHITE 65

What Is the *New Astrology?*

The New Astrology compares Western signs to Chinese signs and comes up with 144 *new* signs. If you are a Sagittarius and were born in 1949, then you are a Sagittarius/Ox. Simple. Take your regular, familiar astrological sign and match it with the animal sign of the year you were born. Now you have your New astrological sign.

Everybody has a dual nature. Some people are naturally greedy and grasping about money. But surprise! These same people can be generous to a fault in emotional ways, strewing sentiment and affection on their entourage like Santa Claus on a gift binge. People are complicated. They baffle us with their contradictory behavior. We even confuse ourselves with our own haunting ambivalences. How come you get along with Jack and care so much about him when in fact he gets on your nerves? Jack has an abrasive personality. You know that. But you can't help liking the guy. He fascinates you. Why? It's a dilemma. With a solution.

In order to understand your attraction for the difficult Jack, so as to comprehend the opacities of your own soul, by yourself, without the aid of a shrink or a psychiatrist, all you have to do is read *The New Astrology*, apply it to your day-to-day life, and you're off and running.

Why Does the New Astrology Work?

The New Astrology work attempts to help us understand human behavior within the universe through the "marriage" of occidental and oriental astrologies. By blending the western Sun Signs with the Chinese Animal signs, we can view many more sides of a person's character than we do with a single type of astrology.

The Chinese have divided time differently from us Westerners. Whereas we have 100-year centuries, the Chinese have periods of sixty years. We divide our centuries into ten decades. The Chinese divide their sixty-year spans into "dozencades" or twelve-year periods.

In the West, we divide our year up twelve times by its moons. Each 28- to 30-day month has its own astrological name. Every year our cycle begins anew. In the East, each year within the twelve-year dozencade has its own astrological name. At the end of each twelve-year period the Chinese cycle begins anew.

The twelve occidental months have celestial sign names: *Aries, Taurus, Gemini, Cancer, Leo, Virgo, Libra, Scorpio, Sagittarius, Capricorn, Aquarius, Pisces*. The twelve oriental years have animal sign names: *Rat, Ox, Tiger, Cat, Dragon, Snake, Horse,*

Goat, Monkey, Rooster, Dog, Pig. In both cases the astrological sign name refers to the character of people born under its influence.

So, in fact, everybody in the world has not just one but two main astrological signs. A Western "month" sign and an Oriental "year" sign. One sign is complementary to the other. Taken together, they show us more about the individual than either one can on its own. In the New Astrology, if someone is born in Aries and is also born in a Horse year, that person's New Astrology sign is *Aries/Horse*. Aries/Horses, as you will see, are not the same as Aries/Cats or Aries/Tigers.

There are 144 (12x12) New Astrology signs. Each is a combined East/West sign. The point of this exercise is to refine our understanding of human nature. Through the New Astrology we can learn to get along better with our friends, family and loved ones. We can find out why we tend not to harmonize with certain people. We can improve our knowledge of them, and of ourselves.

What is this book about?

This book is about **LIBRA**. All 12 kinds of Libra. We begin with the Libra/Rat and end with the Libra/Pig. But before we discover all twelve types of Libra, let's look closely at the Libra sign's qualities and faults.

LIBRA	**Dates**	September 24 to October 23
	Ruler	Venus
	Element	Air
	Quality	Cardinal
	Characteristics	Justice, Aesthetics, Charm, Gentility, Equilibrium, Idealism
	Sins	Quarrelsomeness, Manipulation, Indecision, Procrastination, Self-indulgence, Talkativeness

Have you ever met a person who seems to find everything horrid wonderful and everything wonderful horrid? Have you ever known anyone who finds hidden beauty and grace in people you wouldn't want to take the bus with? Do you know a person who always invariably and constantly alters his or her viewpoint to suit the moment? If the answer to these questions is "yes," you probably know a Libran.

Faced with conflict, Libra never exhibits cowardice. Nor does Libra charge ahead willy-nilly with guns blazing. Instead, Libra attempts to establish negotiations. Libra wants to settle things amicably. Consider first one side, then the other. Libra says, "Don't be too quick to judge people on their face value. Give it time." In fact, by the time Libra has finished flitting from one side of the argument to the other and back forty billion times, the war is very often over.

Libra knows that life is loaded with undercurrents of evil and mined with trouble spots. But the Libran attitude is "Why look for the bad things? Why consider the evil and wretched side of life? Let's put up another watercolor or run out and buy ourselves a lovely new negligee. You'll see. We'll all feel much, much better."

Librans themselves always try to remain on an even keel. They soothe the ill-tempered and cause raging rivers of dissension to flatten out and run smoothly. By means of their good humor and fine sense of what is pleasurable, Librans urge us gently along toward human understanding, beauty and righteousness.

Yet, Librans are capable of being annoyingly argumentative It seems out of character, but there it is. Sometimes the gentle, diplomat needles others. He doesn't want to win arguments. Just wants to find out what you're thinking. Head him off at the pass. Caress the picky Libra's forehead with dollars soaked in Givrey Chambertin.

Librans love luxe. They surround themselves with prettiness and seem to require a comfortable, well-designed frame in which to picture themselves happy. Because of this excessive desire for "the finer things," Librans, if they are sufficiently well looked after, might grow lazy. Perhaps it is unjust to say this as Librans are capable of hard work and tend to be serious about it. But in an ambience of charm and gentility, the Libran revels. In rustic or sparse surroundings the Libran feels cold and longs to return to the land of fashion and folderol.

I have always felt that Librans talked too much. This opinion may be misguided. But still, I do find when I meet Librans for the first time that they have this annoying tendency to over-relate, to recount their life stories and all the details complete with sufferings and losses, injustices and wrongdoings, fears and doubts in Technicolor and Cinemascope. What I want to say to them is "Hey, maybe I don't want to know about every hard-boiled egg you ever ate." Hardly the strong silent type, Libra is placid (except when in a steaming rage) but blabby.

Libras are not in a hurry, nor do they think other people ought to be. My Libra mother asked me once, "Why do you wash the dishes so fast?" I answered tersely, "Because I *hate* washing the dishes." "Oh," she said, with a pretty smile out of which I expected to see a flower grow. "I see." She didn't see at all. But to keep the peace ..

Now to the **Chinese Calendar and Signs.** Here is a mere sampling of the character of the Chinese Animal signs you will encounter in this book. For all the information on Chinese Animal signs please get my e-book THE NEW CHINESE ASTROLOGY© at: http://www.suzannewhite.com

The Chinese Calendar (1900 to 2020)

Year	Sign	Element	Year begins	Year ends
1900	Rat	Metal	01/31/1900	02/18/1901
1901	Ox	Metal	02/19/1901	02/07/1902
1902	Tiger	Water	02/08/1902	01/28/1903
1903	Cat	Water	01/29/1903	02/15/1904
1904	Dragon	Wood	02/16/1904	02/03/1905
1905	Snake	Wood	02/04/1905	01/24/1906
1906	Horse	Fire	01/25/1906	02/12/1907
1907	Goat	Fire	02/13/1907	02/01/1908
1908	Monkey	Earth	02/02/1908	01/21/1909
1909	Rooster	Earth	01/22/1909	02/09/1910
1910	Dog	Metal	02/10/1910	01/29/1911
1911	Pig	Metal	01/30/1911	02/17/1912
1912	Rat	Water	02/18/1912	02/05/1913
1913	Ox	Water	02/06/1913	01/25/1914
1914	Tiger	Wood	01/26/1914	02/13/1915
1915	Cat	Wood	02/14/1915	02/02/1916
1916	Dragon	Fire	02/03/1916	01/22/1917
1917	Snake	Fire	01/23/1917	02/10/1918
1918	Horse	Earth	02/11/1918	01/31/1919
1919	Goat	Earth	02/01/1919	02/19/1920
1920	Monkey	Metal	02/20/1920	02/07/1921
1921	Rooster	Metal	02/08/1921	01/27/1922
1922	Dog	Water	01/28/1922	02/15/1923
1923	Pig	Water	02/16/1923	02/04/1924

1924	Rat	Wood	02/05/1924	01/23/1925
1925	Ox	Wood	01/24/1925	02/12/1926
1926	Tiger	Fire	02/13/1926	02/01/1927
1927	Cat	Fire	02/02/1927	01/22/1928
1928	Dragon	Earth	01/23/1928	02/09/1929
1929	Snake	Earth	02/10/1929	01/29/1930
1930	Horse	Metal	01/30/1930	02/16/1931
1931	Goat	Metal	02/17/1931	02/05/1932
1932	Monkey	Water	02/06/1932	01/25/1933
1933	Rooster	Water	01/26/1933	02/13/1934
1934	Dog	Wood	02/14/1934	02/03/1935
1935	Pig	Wood	02/04/1935	01/23/1936
1936	Rat	Fire	01/24/1936	02/10/1937
1937	Ox	Fire	02/11/1937	01/30/1938
1938	Tiger	Earth	01/31/1938	02/18/1939
1939	Cat	Earth	02/19/1939	02/07/1940
1940	Dragon	Metal	02/08/1940	01/26/1941
1941	Snake	Metal	01/27/1941	02/14/1942
1942	Horse	Water	02/15/1942	02/04/1943
1943	Goat	Water	02/05/1943	01/24/1944
1944	Monkey	Wood	01/25/1944	02/12/1945
1945	Rooster	Wood	02/13/1945	02/01/1946
1946	Dog	Fire	02/02/1946	01/21/1947
1947	Pig	Fire	01/22/1947	02/09/1948
1948	Rat	Earth	02/10/1948	01/28/1949
1949	Ox	Earth	01/29/1949	02/16/1950
1950	Tiger	Metal	02/17/1950	02/05/1951
1951	Cat	Metal	02/06/1951	01/26/1952

1952	Dragon	Water	01/27/1952	02/13/1953
1953	Snake	Water	02/14/1953	02/02/1954
1954	Horse	Wood	02/03/1954	01/23/1955
1955	Goat	Wood	01/24/1955	02/11/1956
1956	Monkey	Fire	02/12/1956	01/30/1957
1957	Rooster	Fire	01/31/1957	02/17/1958
1958	Dog	Earth	02/18/1958	02/07/1959
1959	Pig	Earth	02/08/1959	01/27/1960
1960	Rat	Metal	01/28/1960	02/14/1961
1961	Ox	Metal	02/15/1961	02/04/1962
1962	Tiger	Water	02/05/1962	01/24/1963
1963	Cat	Water	01/25/1963	02/12/1964
1964	Dragon	Wood	02/13/1964	02/01/1965
1965	Snake	Wood	02/02/1965	01/20/1966
1966	Horse	Fire	01/21/1966	02/08/1967
1967	Goat	Fire	02/09/1967	01/29/1968
1968	Monkey	Earth	01/30/1968	02/16/1969
1969	Rooster	Earth	02/17/1969	02/05/1970
1970	Dog	Metal	02/06/1970	01/26/1971
1971	Pig	Metal	01/27/1971	02/14/1972
1972	Rat	Water	02/15/1972	02/02/1973
1973	Ox	Water	02/03/1973	01/22/1974
1974	Tiger	Wood	01/23/1974	02/10/1975
1975	Cat	Wood	02/11/1975	01/30/1976
1976	Dragon	Fire	01/31/1976	02/17/1977
1977	Snake	Fire	02/18/1977	02/06/1978
1978	Horse	Earth	02/07/1978	01/27/1979
1979	Goat	Earth	01/28/1979	02/15/1980

1980	Monkey	Metal	02/16/1980	02/04/1981
1981	Rooster	Metal	02/05/1981	01/24/1982
1982	Dog	Water	01/25/1982	02/12/1983
1983	Pig	Water	02/13/1983	02/01/1984
1984	Rat	Wood	02/02/1984	02/19/1985
1985	Ox	Wood	02/20/1985	02/08/1986
1986	Tiger	Fire	02/09/1986	01/28/1987
1987	Cat	Fire	01/29/1987	02/16/1988
1988	Dragon	Earth	02/17/1988	02/05/1989
1989	Snake	Earth	02/06/1989	02/26/1990
1990	Horse	Metal	01/27/1990	02/14/1991
1991	Goat	Metal	02/15/1991	02/03/1992
1992	Monkey	Water	02/04/1992	01/22/1993
1993	Rooster	Water	01/23/1993	02/09/1994
1994	Dog	Wood	02/10/1994	01/30/1995
1995	Pig	Wood	01/31/1995	02/18/1996
1996	Rat	Fire	02/19/1996	02/06/1997
1997	Ox	Fire	02/07/1997	01/27/1998
1998	Tiger	Earth	01/28/1998	02/15/1999
1999	Cat	Earth	02/16/1999	02/04/2000
2000	Dragon	Metal	02/05/2000	01/23/2001
2001	Snake	Metal	01/24/2001	02/11/2002
2002	Horse	Water	02/12/2002	01/31/2003
2003	Goat	Water	02/01/2003	01/21/2004
2004	Monkey	Wood	01/22/2004	02/08/2005
2005	Rooster	Wood	02/09/2005	01/28/2006
2006	Dog	Fire	01/29/2006	02/17/2007
2007	Pig	Fire	02/18/2007	02/06/2008

2008	Rat	Earth	02/07/2008	01/25/2009
2009	Ox	Earth	01/26/2009	02/13/2010
2010	Tiger	Metal	02/14/2010	02/02/2011
2011	Cat	Metal	02/03/2011	01/22/2012
2012	Dragon	Water	01/23/2012	02/09/2013
2013	Snake	Water	02/10/2013	01/30/2014
2014	Horse	Wood	01/31/2014	02/18/2015
2015	Goat	Wood	02/19/2015	02/07/2016
2016	Monkey	Fire	02/08/2016	01/27/2017
2017	Rooster	Fire	01/28/2017	02/15/2018
2018	Dog	Earth	02/16/2018	02/04/2019
2019	Pig	Earth	02/05/2019	01/24/2020

RATS ARE:

*Seductive • Energetic • Of good counsel • Charming
Meticulous • Sociable • Jolly • Persistent • Humorous • Intellectual
Lovable • Sentimental • Generous • Honest*

BUT THEY CAN ALSO BE:

*Profiteering • Manipulative • Agitated • Gamblers
Greedy • Petty • Suspicious • Disquiet • Tiresome
Destructive • Power-hungry*

OXEN ARE:

*Patient • Hard-working • Familial • Methodical • Loners • Leaders
Proud • Equilibriated • Reserved • Precise • Confidence-inspiring • Eloquent
Self-sacrificing • Original • Silent • Long-suffering • Strong • Tenacious*

BUT THEY CAN ALSO BE:

*Slow • Loutish • Stubborn • Sore losers • Authoritarian
Conventional • Resistant to change • Misunderstood
Rigid • Vindictive • Jealous*

TIGERS ARE:

*Hugely generous • Well-mannered • Courageous • Self-assured • Leaders
Protectors • Honorable • Noble • Active • Liberal-minded • Magnetic • Lucky Strong
Authoritative Sensitive • Deep-thinking • Passionate • Venerable*

BUT THEY CAN ALSO BE:

*Undisciplined • Uncompromising • Vain • Rash
In constant danger • Disobedient • Hasty • Hotheaded
Stubborn • Disrespectful of rules • Quarrelsome*

CAT/RABBITS ARE:

*Discreet • Refined • Virtuous • Social • Tactful
Unflappable • Sensitive • Companionable • Solicitous • Ambitious
Gifted • Forgiving • Prudent • Traditional • Hospitable • Clever*

BUT THEY CAN ALSO BE:

*Old-fashioned • Pedantic • Thin-skinned
Devious • Aloof • Private • Dilettantish • Fainthearted
Squeamish • Hypochondriacal*

DRAGONS ARE:

*Scrupulous • Sentimental • Enthusiastic • Intuitive • Shrewd
Tenacious • Healthy • Influential • Vital • Generous • Spirited
Captivating • Artistic • Admirable • Lucky • Successful • Autonomous*

BUT THEY CAN ALSO BE:

*Disquiet • Stubborn • Willful • Demanding
Irritable • Loud-mouthed • Malcontent • Other-worldly
Impetuous • Infatuate • Judgmental*

SNAKES ARE:

*Wise • Cultivated • Cerebral • Accommodating • Intuitive
Attractive • Amusing • Lucky • Sympathetic • Elegant • Soft-spoken
Well-bred • Compassionate • Philosophical • Calm • Decisive*

BUT THEY CAN ALSO BE:

*Ostentatious • Sore losers • Tight-fisted
Extravagant • Presumptuous • Possessive • Vengeful
Self-critical • Phlegmatic • Lazy • Fickle*

HORSES ARE:

Amiable • Eloquent • Skillful • Self-possessed
Quick-witted • Athletic • Entertaining • Charming • Independent
Powerful • Hard-working • Jolly • Sentimental • Frank • Sensual

BUT THEY CAN ALSO BE:

Selfish • Weak • Hotheaded • Ruthless
Rebellious • Pragmatic • Foppish • Tactless
Impatient • Unfeeling • Predatory

GOATS ARE:

Elegant • Creative • Intelligent • Well-mannered • Sweet-natured
Tasteful • Inventive • Homespun • Persevering • Lovable • Delicate
Artistic • Amorous • Malleable • Altruistic • Peace-loving

BUT THEY CAN ALSO BE:

Pessimistic • Fussbudgets • Dissatisfied
Capricious • Intrusive • Undisciplined • Dependent
Irresponsible • Unpunctual • Insecure

MONKEYS ARE:

Acutely intelligent • Witty • Inventive • Affable • Problem-solvers
Independent • Skillful business people • Achievers • Enthusiastic
Lucid • Nimble • Passionate • Youthful • Fascinating • Clever

BUT THEY CAN ALSO BE:

Tricky tacticians • Vain • Dissimulators
Opportunistic • Long-winded • Not all that trustworthy
Unfaithful • Adolescent • Unscrupulous

ROOSTERS ARE:

*Frank • Vivacious • Courageous • Resourceful • Attractive
Talented • Generous • Sincere • Enthusiastic • Conservative • Industrious
Stylish • Amusing • Contemplative • Popular • Adventurous • Self-assured*

BUT THEY CAN ALSO BE:

*Nit-pickers • Braggarts • Quixotic
Mistrusful • Acerb • Short-sighted • Didactic
Pompous • Pedantic • Spendthrift • Brazen*

DOGS ARE:

*Magnanimous • Courageous • Noble • Loyal • Devoted
Attentive • Selfless • Faithful • Modest • Altruistic • Prosperous
Philosophical • Respectable • Discreet • Dutiful • Lucid • Intelligent*

BUT THEY CAN ALSO BE:

*Disquiet • Guarded • Introverted
Defensive • Critical • Pessimistic • Florbidding
Cynical • Stubborn • Moralizing*

PIGS ARE:

*Obliging • Loyal • Scrupulous • Indulgent • Truthful
Impartial • Intelligent • Sincere • Sociable • Thorough • Cultured
Sensual • Decisive • Peaceable • Loving • Profound • Sensitive*

BUT THEY CAN ALSO BE:

*Naive • Defenseless • Insecure • Sardonic • Epicurean
Noncompetitive • Willful • Gullible • Earthy • Easy prey*

The New Astrology

LIBRA	RAT

JUSTICE	QUARRELSOMENESS	INTUITION	DISSIMULATION
AESTHETICS	MANIPULATION	ATTRACTIVENESS	EXTRAVAGANCE
CHARM	PROCRASTINATION	DISCRETION	LAZINESS
GENTILITY	SELF-INDULGENCE	SAGACITY	CUPIDITY
EQUILIBRIUM	INDECISION	CLAIRVOYANCE	PRESUMPTION
IDEALISM	TALKATIVENESS	COMPASSION	EXCLUSIVITY

"I balance"

Air, Venus, Cardinal

"I sense"

Negative Fire, Yang

A gifted combination, to say the least. Libra/Rat lives in a perpetual state of hopefulness. Libra/Rat wants to break the bank at Monte Carlo, star in a play on Broadway and… write a bestseller. Further, they'd like to beget—or better still, be—the president of the United States. And when she is finished with those incidentals, she would like to take time out to win the Nobel Prize.

Libra/Rats are almost self-destructively ambitious. They cannot leave the quest for supremacy alone. As their truest gifts lie within the realms of poetry and fancy, the usual Rat pursuit of power—that is, power over others—rarely, if ever, enters their tense little claws. These people are also extremely gabby and exhaustingly communicative. They want to tell it all, all the time and in the most excruciating detail.

It's easy to enjoy a Libra/Rat's company. They are affable and open. They are curious about others and show quick compassion for their interlocutors' problems and sorrows. Libra/Rat is a fascinating sign. These subjects intrigue and plot and gossip their whole lives away. They behave in a convoluted and complex fashion. They are both avaricious and generous. They like to have money so they can give it away to those they deem worthy. They are idealistic and extreme.

Libra/Rats want to dominate. Yet they are not nasty or authoritarian people. Their method of controlling others is unusual. Libra/Rats control through sweetness. They endear themselves through their apparent guilelessness to those they admire and seek the company of. By this enticing means, the Libra/Rat manages to become indispensable to those who love him or her. Once you have a Libra/Rat as a friend you will have no end of real companionship. But neither will you be alone—ever again.

Librans and Rats both tend to talk out their inner feelings as a method of problem solving. Neither sign is violent. Neither personality suffers from stodginess. As a result, there is a quality of lightness that surrounds this character, of amiability and an almost childlike candor. Thing is, the attitude is just that. The overt sincerity we encounter in this person is a bit of an act. Libra/Rats pretend to be simple folk. They come on plainspoken and "How dee do." But watch out. Before you know it you'll be outmaneuvered by this wily bundle of sunshine.

Libra/Rat is painfully sensitive to others and is therefore capable of inspiring an audience to follow his high-blown ideals. Librans born in Rat years have a remarkable memory for detail and a giant capacity for creation. Both Rat and Libra are deeply rooted in tradition. Customs and religion die hard in the minds of these exacting creatures.

For a feisty Rat person to be born under the aesthetic sign of Libra is indeed a blessing. Libra's gentility tames the Rat's occasional harshness. The oft-prejudiced Rat personality benefits from Libra's sense of justice and picks up subtlety in the bargain. The combination certainly doesn't want for maneuvering tactics, nor does it lack charisma.

Love

The Libra/Rat takes his or her feelings very seriously. Emotion is, to the Libra/Rat, a commodity that he or she dispenses with great care and discrimination. Once he has taken to a sweetheart, the plot very definitely thickens. Romance is not something to be trifled with where Libra/Rat is concerned. Moreover, he is never unfaithful to love itself—only to his lover or mistress.

If you have fallen in love one of these crafty beauties, I suggest you invest in some velvet gloves. "Handle With Care" is stamped all over the tenderness center of Libra/Rat. This is a vocal lover. He or she will come on strong. The initial impact will surely be noteworthy. You cannot ignore this effervescent character. Like fine champagne, this person requires a little stirring up to get rid of the excess bubbly. Then, sip slowly and enjoy.

Compatibilities

You are fatally attracted by Geminis, Leos, Sagittarians and Aquarians. Narrow the field of choice from among these signs to Monkey people. They not only appeal to you but they have something to offer you in return. You like Dragons and Oxen, so choose them, if you prefer, from the same sign groups as the Monkeys. Leo/Dragons are a bit much for your delicate equilibrium, so leave that one alone if you can. I don't believe you can be happy forever with an Aries, Cancer or Capricorn/Horse—or any other Horse subject, for that matter. Cats born in Cancer or Capricorn are too fearful to stand by you in times of trouble.

Home and Family

Nobody loves a cozy atmosphere like a Libran born Rat. Thing is, this person is not expert at creating said ambience and needs a homier soul to get furnishings and decor together. If it were up to the Rat/Libra, he would call in a decorator and have him build everything from some grandiose Rat/Libra-inspired plan. He's not much of a putterer, this Rat. And he isn't really drawn to things noncerebral, like model building model airplanes or fixing lawnmowers. This person's home is only as beautiful as his decorator is talented. He doesn't see the point of getting his hands dirty with do-it-yourself projects like painting ceiling and plastering walls.

As a parent this person is reliable and responsible, warm-hearted and sincere, communicative in the extreme and not all that lenient. Libra/Rats want their kids to excel at everything. They take their children's victories (and their failures) personally. Rat/Libras are essentially social parents and love being part of everything their children do. From the PTA bake sale to the Little League picnic committee, you can count on a Libra/Rat parent to be there with bells on.

The Libra/Rat child is a hypersensitive chatterbox. He or she will probably respond ticklishly to criticism and have a hard time accepting disapproval from parents or teachers. Personality is a definite plus in Libra/Rat kids, so of course they will be popular among their peers. Encourage this child to read. Words delight the Libra/Rat and may indeed furnish him with a sound future metier.

Profession

To stem the flow of words emanating from the Libra/Rat is to cruelly hinder his or her development. Libra/Rats think aloud. They are supremely talented in all work involving communication, persuasion and sociability. They can be both meddling and quarrelsome and need occasional squelching from superiors to stay in line. Libra/Rat is a dickerer over prices and understands the value of a shekel. He or she is idealistic about career matters. Libra/Rats don't see themselves as any small potatoes. They're intellectual as well as dynamic.

Rats born in Libra make less partial bosses than one might think. Libra loosens the Rat's tight grip on his underlings, making him more altruistic and diplomatic. Oh, yes. He does blab a lot. But then better a blathering boss than the old strong silent mean type. If you aim to employ this fellow gainfully, you'd better make sure he works in a closet without telephones. He is very easily distracted by communication with co-workers and can be the king of the water cooler crowd. Libra/Rat is, however, efficient and well worth his weight in phone bill when it comes to telephone skills.

Good career choices for Libra/Rat are: writer, advertising executive, teacher, composer, salesperson, journalist, entertainer, switchboard operator, psychologist, preacher.

Some famous Libra/Rats: T. S. Eliot, Thomas Wolfe, Eugene O'Neill, Truman Capote, Jimmy Carter, Jim Henson, Avril Lavigne, Charlton Heston, Eminem, Gwyneth Paltrow, Helen Hayes, Jean-Claude Van Damme, Jean Piat, Lotte Lenya, Marcello Mastroianni, Nicole Croisille, Stephen Bechtel.

The New Astrology

LIBRA	OX

JUSTICE	QUARRELSOMENESS	STUBBORNNESS	INTEGRITY
AESTHETICS	MANIPULATION	STRENGTH OF PURPOSE	BIGOTRY
CHARM	PROCRASTINATION	ELOQUENCE	PLODDING
GENTILITY	SELF-INDULGENCE	STANDOFFISHNESS	DILIGENCE
EQUILIBRIUM	INDECISION	INNOVATION	BIAS
IDEALISM	TALKATIVENESS	VINDICTIVENESS	STABILITY

"I balance" — *"I sense"*

Air, Venus, Cardinal — *Negative Water, Yin*

Beauty and the Beast. This subject is a veritable storm of contradiction. Every detail must be perfect, every line straight and every flaw concealed. Weakness must be routed. Sloth eradicated. Yet, under this foil of faultlessness, Libra/Ox hides a secret. On the strict surface, Libra/Ox is efficiency and power, example and security. Underneath? An anthill of conflicting emotions. Purity charms this sterling character. He claims not to want any messes about. He protests he needs calm and cannot live in turmoil, Yet, Libra/Oxen are forever getting themselves involved in emotional scrapes. Even though they seem to be above it all, they take in strays. They seek out madness. They are magnetized by complexity.

Librans born in Ox years are basically gentle people. They are addicted to beauty and cannot resist following this penchant. Their dream is perfection in life design. Clean, well-mannered children and pets. Lovely surroundings. Soft music playing in the background. Sumptuous haute cuisine, overflowing Louis XV dining tables, a sensible, fascinating mate who does Libra/Ox proud in the world at large, and even well-behaved in-laws.

But Libra/Oxen also fear that just as they have achieved this precious house of cards, tied up their own prettily wrapped package, the slightest breeze will certainly come along and destroy it.

Disappointment is the enemy of Libra/Oxen. They are constantly finding others less impeccable than they would like. They are often deceived by those they love, and yet, time and again they come back for more. If certain configurations repeatedly disillusion us, we ought to avoid those patterns. But the Libra/Ox refuses. Stubbornly, and with no apparent sense of what has gone before or what is to come, Libra/Ox wakes up after monstrous bouts with chagrin and disenchantment, staggers to his feet and starts all over again. This time it will be different, hopes the earnest Libra/Ox. And this time is always exactly the same. Only the sets change.

Libra/Ox people make eloquent raconteurs. When a Libra/Ox tells you the tales of his repeated woes and how he has been battered and buffeted by life and friends and family, you are riveted to your seat. What? This calm, unassuming, ingenuous and simple sort has been involved in such weirdness? Such baroque emotions have lived in that homespun person's heart? Frankly, when you see a Libra/Ox in all of his or her glorious homeliness, you can only wonder where all the complexity fits in.

Libra/Ox, it goes without saying, is a family-dependent person. He or she will not be much of a party-goer or social butterfly. Libra/Ox prefers home (and all of its relatively manageable embroilments) to the scatty and unclean outside world. Sometimes, if you're lucky, this Ox (because he is born Libra) will have acquired a certain distance from his own emotions. Then, with the natural eloquence given him or her at birth, this character can become exceedingly humorous.

These folks know how to use words wisely. Libra is naturally talkative but not always artful. Ox, on the contrary, doesn't say much but what he says is usually skillfully articulated What results in the Libra/Ox personality is sometimes known as the "gift of gab"—a real talent for entertaining with words.

Love

The province of romance in this person's existence is densely populated, to say the least. If you consider the variety and disparity of emotional influences alive in this subject's spirit, you will begin to comprehend just how overgrown is the sentimental acreage behind his superficially stolid facade. This native is deceptively frolicsome as a love partner. Inside, he or she is a roiling cauldron of emotional hang-ups and demands. In love situations, Libra/Ox is both quarrelsome and manipulative.

One of the compensations for the difficulties of cohabitation with the Libra/Ox is that you will always be guaranteed a safe and secure home. Moreover, should you wish to, you are allowed to appear to be thoroughly insane. Libra/Ox will love you more for your eccentricities, your oddball beliefs and your own complex miseries. Remember, however, that the Libra/Ox's stability is only skin deep. Act crazy if you want. But keep your head about you. The Libra/Ox, in his lust for experience, may be needing a wise second opinion.

Compatibilities

Your natural partners usually live in Gemini, Leo, Sagittarius and Aquarius. Snakes born in these signs are wise choices for you. You also get on with Rats born in Leo, Sagittarius and Aquarius. Gemini and Sagittarius/Roosters suit you well, as do Roosters born in both Leo and Aquarius. There now, you have quite a wide choice, don't you? But beware! Aries, Cancer and Capricorn/Tigers don't inspire you with their flashy causes. Nor do Cancer/Dragons, Horses and Monkeys.

Home and Family

"United we stand, divided we fall" should be the Libra/Ox's motto. This person's devotion to the unit, the cause, the order, the system and of course the family is exemplary. As head of a household he's at his most content. Libra/Ox likes to think of himself as the most benevolent, generous and philanthropic despot who ever lived on this earth. You, as a card-carrying member of his clan, should be honored to have him as your leader. Yawn.

I've already mentioned the secret furbelows that this person prefers in his home decor. No matter how roughly countrified his home may appear, this person will have a "lace curtain" mentality. He likes frippery and his tastes run to the gaudy. Nowhere, in fact, is the Libra/Ox schizophrenia so obvious as in his home. The heavy and cumbersome is always side by side with the frivolous. That's Libra/Ox: a porcelain teacup in a heavy ceramic saucer.

As parents these people are demanding and loving. They cling to rigid standards and yet indulge their kids emotionally. The Libra/Ox child will be both dutiful and fanciful. This kid needs security and a sense of teamwork. He or she will respond well to schoolwork, as such a child is always looking for stability and order. Don't be surprised by your Libra/Ox child's solemnity. On the other hand, don't be shocked by this kid's desire to tie bows on the Doberman's ears. They like things pretty.

Profession

Librans born in Ox years tend to achieve in the outside world. They have a taste for regular hours and can adhere to strict schedules, meet deadlines with ease and deliver the goods where work is concerned. They are diligent and (exceptional for Oxen) very cooperative. Libran Ox people are even diplomatic. They nit-pick a lot but are endowed with extraordinary strength and won't hesitate to take on the toughest jobs in any work situation.

I'm not sure I'd like to have a Libra/Ox boss. They are such models of good behavior on the surface that I should always feel diminished by comparison. Libra/Ox rules by example. This person is also a model employee. He doesn't balk at even the least gratifying tasks. Moreover, when he's on his way up, he's always willing to put in overtime. He'll be stubborn. But essentially he wants to cooperate.

You can impress him by your own irreproachable behavior. Some good careers for Libra/Oxen are: writer, preacher, newscaster, educator, antique dealer, social worker.

Famous Libra/Oxen: Chester Alan Arthur, Art Buchwald, Gore Vidal, Benjamin Netanyahu (Israel), Bruce Springsteen, Ed Sullivan, Enrico Fermi, Heather Locklear, J.P. Elkabach, Margaret Thatcher, Steve Young, Temple Fielding, Wynton Marsalis.

The New Astrology

LIBRA		TIGER	
JUSTICE	QUARRELSOMENESS	FERVOR	IMPETUOSITY
AESTHETICS	MANIPULATION	BRAVERY	HOTHEADEDNESS
CHARM	PROCRASTINATION	MAGNETISM	DISOBEDIENCE
GENTILITY	SELF-INDULGENCE	GOOD LUCK	SWAGGER
EQUILIBRIUM	INDECISION	BENEVOLENCE	INTEMPERANCY
IDEALISM	TALKATIVENESS	AUTHORITY	ITINERANCY

"I balance"

Air, Venus, Cardinal

"I watch"

Positive Wood, Yang

An original if there ever was one, the Libra/Tiger is unforgettably winning. This person wants to impress and please you. You may react coldly, but more likely you will warm to the Tigerish Libran charisma and want to know more—much more—about him. Attractive? My gawd. These people emit personal magnetism rays that dance all over their countenances. Libra/Tiger seems perpetually on the brink of bursting out laughing. It's adorable. It's fascinating. And it is mighty perilous for the heartstrings.

In its raw state, personal magnetism doesn't pay the rent. There is not a lot for which you can barter a pound of intangible cuteness. But somehow these people charm the very pants off the world, invite respect and recruit followers with a mere snap of their fingers. I am not, decidedly not, suggesting that the Libra/Tiger is a phony. He doesn't flit about picking up groupies on a whim. The Libra/Tiger understands the value of a hard day's work and is willing to put in his time on all manner of projects. But the most arresting quality that this native possesses is self-assured magic. It will take him or her very far.

Libra/Tigers have a finely developed sense of justice and care deeply about doing good. They are, however, exceedingly irreverent. Systems and social conventions, outdated traditions and even up-to-date laws strike the Libra/

Tiger as inapplicable to a person of his lofty stature. Libra/Tiger feels as though by virtue of his own natural superiority, he knows best for himself and for those he advises and leads. He is almost incapable of acquiescing to play by the rules, but is luckily endowed with just enough Libran balance to keep him (most of the time) out of jail.

In a way, for a Libra to be born Tiger is troublesome. Libra is attracted to the "feminine" in life. He or she aims at drawing the beauty out of every encounter and is, on principle, a peace-seeker. As we already know, Tigers don't care about peace. Tigers care about truth. Tigers care about ideals. Tigers care about Tigers. This causes some basic disparity in the Libra/Tiger nature. That silly Tiger whose need for security is nil and who couldn't care less about social graces or bother with frills living inside the genteel Libra's head drives the Libra to distraction.

But distracted this subject does not remain for long. Libra/Tiger is dauntless in her search for a place in the sun, a name for herself, a star in the heavens of renown. This person's stabs at fame and fortune are many. And she often succeeds brilliantly at what she's set out to do. She is hotheaded and sometimes even foolish. But Libra/Tigers have a spark of refinement and a nose for the elegant that serves to scrape them off the woodwork and back into the good graces of whomever their hotheadedness has offended.

The Libra/Tiger's specialty is the stroke of genius. Whether it be in the realm of global politics or the more mundane business of throwing a Sunday brunch in honor of nothing more sophisticated than a family birthday, this person has an unbeatable touch. It's charismatic, yes. But it's also intelligent. Libra/Tiger has innate brilliance in his sign. Nothing he puts his hand to will be ordinary. It can be very wicked. But it will never be banal.

Love

Librans born in Tiger years make excellent mates. They are sufficiently sexual, but they are not dependent on sex for their equilibrium and are therefore one step ahead of the rest of the pack. For a Tiger this person is sweet-natured and sentimental. He's vulnerable, too, so don't go being harsh with this darling. The presence of this dashing person always lends enchantment to romance. They are rash and argumentative. But they are fun to fight with.

If you have the good luck to know one of these delectable creatures or even to be in love with one, I envy you. Libra/Tigers are among the world's swaggerers. They know how to dress. They carry off everything they try with panache and aplomb. They swashbuckle. If you want to keep this person in your home, you must provide him with permanent opportunities for creating a splash. This person wants notoriety in his own circle and even in a cosmic way. You will best please him or her by staying out of the path, never making disobliging comments and secretly, skillfully, advising your loved one to keep his or her mouthiness in check.

Compatibilities

You'll love a Gemini, Leo, Sagittarius or Aquarius born in Horse or Dog years. The harmonies flow naturally with them. Dragons from Sagittarius and Aquarius also hit the spot. You're better off without Aries, Cancer or Capricorn/Cats. You'll have trouble getting along with Aries/Snakes. Capricorn and Cancer/Oxen as well as Goats are taboo.

Home and Family

Dear, dear. What can I say? The Libra/Tiger is a terrible spendthrift about the house. This impulsive charmer adorns his surroundings in an expensive and lavish fashion. "Change those ordinary-looking doorknobs. Get me a golden molding on that picture frame. Put up this embossed satin wallpaper imported from Thailand, and don't forget to allow for at least enough hot water for my three baths per day." Oh, my. It's so luxuriously efficient around the Tiger/Libra house.

As a parent the Libra/Tiger is caring. He or she will be thoughtful with regard to children and enjoy providing the guidance they require. The Libra/Tiger seduces kids like a parental Pied Piper. There's a spirit of cooperation and fairness about the parent-child relationship. Libra/Tiger may not always be available to watch over every detail. But when he or she is around, the time spent with kids is quality time.

Profession

Without hesitation I can say that Libra/Tigers are willing to pitch in and work. They are not shy of dirtying their hands and rarely complain of fatigue. These people are wiry and resistant. They have natural grace and don't hesitate to use their charms for personal betterment. They are not concerned with social climbing unless the "right" people prove somehow useful to them. Tiger/Libras are leaders and don't like to follow. They need a wise staff of advisers, as their weakness is haste.

Of course this person will want to be boss. You would have a hard time persuading him otherwise. As a boss, this character is surprisingly impartial and congenial. Tigers born Libra are fair and square, idealistic even, about how they treat others. They often take unpopular stands and will exact utter loyalty from underlings and associates alike.

As an employee or subordinate, the Libra/Tiger is circumspect and knows how to wait his turn to be boss. He will never accept a subordinate position in life. If he is obliged to, he will simply pine away.

Some career choices for Libra/Tigers are: head of government, clothes designer, decorator, revolutionary, speechwriter, adventurer, philosopher, playwright, entertainer, fundraiser.

Famous Libra/Tigers: Rimbaud, Oscar Wilde, Dwight D. Eisenhower, Thor Heyerdahl, Michel Foucault, Valéry Giscard d'Estaing, Mary McFadden, Ayatollah Khomenei, Chester A. Arthur, Danièle Delorme, Groucho Marx, Howard Rollins, Ray Kroc, Romy Schneider, Susan Anton, Willem Kok (Holland).

The New Astrology

LIBRA

JUSTICE	QUARRELSOMENESS
AESTHETICS	MANIPULATION
CHARM	PROCRASTINATION
GENTILITY	SELF-INDULGENCE
EQUILIBRIUM	INDECISION
IDEALISM	TALKATIVENESS

"I balance"

Air, Venus, Cardinal

CAT / RABBIT

TACT	SECRETIVENESS
FINESSE	SQUEAMISHNESS
VIRTUE	PEDANTRY
PRUDENCE	DILETTANTISM
LONGEVITY	HYPOCHONDRIA
AMBITION	COMPLEXITY

"I retreat"

Negative Wood, Yin

Tasteful, gracious living is the aim of the character born in the double sign of aesthetic appreciation. Librans born in Cat years are stay-at-home, suspicious, squeamish souls. They trust with great difficulty. Libra's discretion about passing quick judgments becomes, in this subject, a near refusal to judge anything or anyone. Libra/Cats hesitate so long before making decisions or committing themselves that they frequently lose their prey.

"Oh, wouldn't he or she make a wonderful mate for So-and-so?" is a question often asked about the Libra/Cat. Outwardly, the calm and delicate, sensible and graceful person we describe here seems to have the makings of a perfect mate. But image is not always reality. Don't forget that when they encounter conflict, Cats slide away. They hate to be confronted. They never attack head on. They simply disappear.

Libra/Cat is the worst kind of slip-slider. He or she will never be held down—not even to a fight! Moreover, the act of hitching their wagon to an ideal or to another human being is practically beyond them. Libra/Cats are the epitome of bewildered indecision. And what's more, they like it that way.

In a very young person, constant vacillation is acceptable. People, these days, seem to spend quite a number of their youthful years "finding" themselves. At thirty, if you haven't found yourself, you might safely deduce that you were not there in the first place, and simply carry on as before. Libra/Cats sometimes die looking for themselves—at age eighty! These people hem and haw. Nothing is ever quite good enough for their refined tastes. So they frequently just stay where they are (even if it's still at home with mother) for want of the pluck to decide to change anything.

Libra/Cat is not stubborn. But if challenged by an emergency decision, he may grow cranky and bad-tempered or deliberately give the impression of somber seriousness so that nobody will call on him. His or her intimate involvement in human interaction is minimal. Yet, because of a very busy social calendar, the Libra/Cat may give just the opposite idea of himself.

Libra/Cats love to entertain. They will go to parties if they are sure to meet celebrities (and name-drop a bit, I might add) or talk animatedly with people who they feel can help them or even just amuse them. But when they leave the party and go home, they draw tight the shutters and crawl down into the safety of home. They cherish their domestic comfort and safeguard it carefully. Libra/Cats are unconscious victims of their need for security. A bohemian lifestyle terrifies them. Lack of certainty freaks them out. No matter how avant-garde a Libra/Cat ever appears, rest assured it's only skin-deep. Libra/Cat is an inveterate bourgeois.

Love

Romantic entanglements delight this tasteful and graceful creature. He or she will often be "in love." Libra/Cats are pleasant and make sweet companions who like to laugh and find beauty everywhere. Like all Librans, the Libra/Cat talks about his love too. They are tender, generous and passionate lovers. But they will have difficulty staying with one person. Are they fickle? Not really. Just indecisive.

If you love a Libra/Cat, the last thing you should do is try to move in with him. You must court them and tease them, giving back some of the medicine they dish out. Don't always be available to them or fawn over their good looks. They need to do the chasing. Keep the ball of yarn just out of reach and watch the Libra/Cat jump for it. The only way to keep a Libra/Cat content is to keep him or her guessing.

Compatibilities

Your closest affinities will be found among Gemini, Leo, Sagittarius and Aquarius people. Within this large family of souls you should look for a Goat, a Dog or a Pig to associate yourself with for romantic purposes. You are not so compatible with Aries/Oxen. You plainly do not get along with Cancer or Capricorn Roosters or Rats. Don't be in a hurry to marry. Take your time.

Before getting engaged, ask everybody you know and trust (not your mother) to have a chat with your choice of life partner. If they think he or she will be good for you, your marriage has a chance to succeed.

Home and Family

The home environment of a Libra/Cat will be refined and traditional, even rich-looking. He favors velvets and satins, stone or marble houses, and furnishes his life in a decorating scheme that allows him to wallow in the "feminine." Big, foam-filled bathtubs, and bouquets of cabbage roses on the wallpaper. Thick carpet up to the tub's rim and comfy robes kept warm by the bathside. And remember, Libra/Cat is not trying to impress anyone but himself.

This person, if he or she ever settles down, will make an okay parent. I say "okay" because parenting is messy and requires plenty of regular confrontation. Fighting is not the Libra/Cat's province at all. This subject will do well with the sweet parts of parenting and eschew the disciplining and mess. Not that Libra/Cat's intentions are not honorable. He or she loves children. But they are so turbulent, aren't they?

The Libra/Cat child will be happiest as an only child. He needs peace and quiet and will shy away from sibling rivalries. If he is the eldest, he can take charge and make sense out of that. Otherwise he'll suffer at the hands of rough and tumble brothers and sisters. Give the Libra/Cat child a refined atmosphere in which to evolve and feel secure. When he comes of age, you will practically have to pry him loose from the nest with a crowbar. If staying home is too comfy, he'll likely never leave.

Profession

Don't expect this person to go rushing out to start his own business, build it into a multimillion-dollar concern and fight his way into the best circles. Libra/Cats are best suited for jobs that allow them to stay at home and work independently. Because of their natural amiability and great strength of character (inside that frail shell is a Mack truck!) they leave an indelible personal impression wherever they go. If a Libra/Cat has to be boss, he will do what he can to slough the real domination off onto someone harsher than himself. He or she will be the sort of boss who hires a "whip" to do the dirty work of seeing that the slaves tote those barges.

Libra/Cat prefers to remain behind the scenes and willingly acts as the brains of any operation. This person has trouble being an employee, too. Libra/Cats don't take direction as gracefully as, for example, they circulate at parties. Their neck hairs bristle when they are treated unfairly or asked to participate in something they see as vulgar or futile. They make a pretty picture, but ought not to be required to "do windows."

Some excellent career choices for Libra/Cats are: bookstore owner, diplomat, translator/interpreter, piano tuner, interior decorator, museum curator, actor/actress (classical theater), writer.

A few famous Libra/Cats: George C. Scott, Arthur Miller, Günter Grass, Brian Boitano, John Cougar Mellencamp, Karen Allen, Kate Winslet, Leo Burnett, Marion Jones, Mark Hamill, Pam Dawber, Pedro Almodóvar, Sting, Vladimir Horowitz.

The New Astrology

LIBRA	DRAGON

JUSTICE	QUARRELSOMENESS	STRENGTH	RIGIDITY
AESTHETICS	MANIPULATION	SUCCESS	MISTRUST
CHARM	PROCRASTINATION	GOOD HEALTH	DISSATISFACTION
GENTILITY	SELF-INDULGENCE	ENTHUSIASM	INFATUATION
EQUILIBRIUM	INDECISION	PLUCK	BRAGGADOCIO
IDEALISM	TALKATIVENESS	SENTIMENTALITY	VOLUBILITY

"I balance"   *"I preside"*

Air, Venus, Cardinal   *Positive Wood, Yang*

The Libra/Dragon is not just anybody. Librans are born manipulators. Dragons tend to be suspicious. Librans seek equilibrium in all matters. Dragons seek to be heard and seen. Neither sign is particularly taciturn. The match is stormy. But despite the tempestuous nature of the Libra/Dragon, he or she will be gifted in carving out unusual destinies.

Many Librans, because they are naturally discreet and seek balance, will know how to put their personality in their pocket—if only for the purpose of not making waves. But here, along comes the thrilling Dragon. Dragons are noisy and know it all. They want to compete and they want to win. I have the impression that in this sign, Libra spends a lot of energy trying to convince his Dragonish volubility to retreat back inside that pocket. And (if you know one of these powerhouses, you will understand what I mean) they don't very often succeed.

Dragons born in Libra get places in life. No matter where they begin, you can be certain they don't end up at square one. These people know the meaning of the adage that you get out of life exactly what you put in. They contribute to their own lives' successes; they make something of themselves and they are not afraid of putting their pride on the line in order to achieve goals.

Libra/Dragon is a creative sign. But even more it is an interpretive sign. People born under this pair of signs combine discernment and energy, idealism and pluck, talkativeness and boastfulness. But never mind. These ebullient folks take us on fabulous trips through their own exciting, imaginative new worlds. They benefit from the unique distinction of self-worship with apparent impunity. Life, for the Libra/Dragon, is there exclusively for his use and pleasure. He has few scruples about taking what he needs and walking away from the rest. His ego is in terrific shape.

Libra/Dragons never give up. They are not dull, hardworking long-sufferers. Oh no. They are brilliant and even fanatical. And when I say they don't give up, I mean they don't even recognize opposition. For the Libra/Dragon, opposition isn't really there. Obstacles melt before them. One wonders, is it magic? And I reply, yes. There is a form of sorcery at work in the Libra/Dragon character. He is self-directed and quite oblivious to the needs of the crowd or the trends of the market. But somehow he knows what to do to please the crowd and to hit that market spot on. He plays hunches—and he wins.

As the center of attention, the Libra/Dragon personality ticks over like a charm. No problem as long as the spotlight is on him. He will expand and amuse and ape and strut and breathe fire endlessly so long as you are tuned in to his channel. Libra/Dragons are even kindly and sentimental and tenderhearted when their egos are being satisfied. But watch out. Don't ever let this person feel that you're about to switch stations. He or she can be real nasty when wronged.

Love

The Libra/Dragon's love life is a patchwork of ups and downs until, after much experimentation, he or she finds the mate of his or her dreams. You see, Libra/Dragons need a built-in audience of one. They have to keep a permanent sounding board around the house. Passion is important to them. But adulation is perhaps more so. Libra/Dragons like to be worshiped. Anything short of homage will leave Libra/Dragon lukewarm.

If you want one of these special little numbers around your house for all time, you've got your hands full. You will definitely save on entertainment costs. You won't need TVs or radios or videos or stereos. Libra/Dragon is the whole show by himself. Your job? Be sensible for your Libra/Dragon. Don't let him or her go too far off the deep end. If you have trouble with him, try pulling on his heartstrings. It's the only method I know of to control this attractive beast's pretentiousness.

Compatibilities

Rats born in Gemini, Leo, Sagittarius or Aquarius will turn you on. You also enjoy harmony with Gemini, Leo and Aquarius/Monkey people. Leo and

Sagittarius/Roosters are good for you, as are lovely Leo/Snake folks. Don't promote any long-standing relationships with Aries, Cancer or Capricorn/Cats or Dogs. And whatever you do, don't get mixed up with a Cancer/Ox. Too stodgy and emotional.

Home and Family

Physically, this person may not be all that smashingly attractive. But he will surround himself with beauty and he will know exactly how he wants his home to be decorated, his clothes to look, his image to project itself on the world. He may choose exotic or exciting furnishings, since he likes to impress. But whatever decor he chooses, its purpose will be to set off the Libra/Dragon to his or her best advantage. Librans born in Dragon years are good at parenting. They like to be looked up to by their offspring. Because of their exceptional view of self and their desire to shine at any cost, Libra/Dragons sometimes have difficulty getting on with their older kids. They don't handle contradiction well. And there is nothing more contradictory than an adolescent child.

Childlessness is common among Libra/Dragons. Many of these complex people, for both personal and professional reasons, prefer not to bother having a family.

Profession

Here is where the Libra/Dragon can really shine. The Libra/Dragon loves his or her career more than anything. Here is where the magic and pizzazz really have a chance to glow. At work, be it a shop or a restaurant, a TV program or a factory production line, when Dragon shows up with Libra in tow, the curtain opens to reveal the great, the one and only—move over world—here comes the king! I don't see this person employed as an underling for long. The patience and rigor factors are extremely low in Libra/ Dragons.

But as a boss, this fellow can be quite loving and warm-hearted. The Libra/Dragon is fervently enthusiastic about himself and his projects and his way of looking at the world. But he's not a mean person. He's not a tough guy. Libra/Dragon wants everything his way, but then his way is, of course, the best way, n'est-ce pas?

Some promising careers for this character are: TV personality, general, entrepreneur, public figure (politician?), airline pilot, shop owner, musician, entertainer, evangelist.

Famous Libra/Dragons: Nietzsche, Sarah Bernhardt, Graham Greene, John Lennon, Rex Reed, Angie Dickinson, Christopher Reeve, Anthony Delon, Jacques Chazot, Pelé, Vladimir Poutin.

The New Astrology

LIBRA	SNAKE

JUSTICE	QUARRELSOMENESS	INTUITION	DISSIMULATION
AESTHETICS	MANIPULATION	ATTRACTIVENESS	EXTRAVAGANCE
CHARM	PROCRASTINATION	DISCRETION	LAZINESS
GENTILITY	SELF-INDULGENCE	SAGACITY	CUPIDITY
EQUILIBRIUM	INDECISION	CLAIRVOYANCE	PRESUMPTION
IDEALISM	TALKATIVENESS	COMPASSION	EXCLUSIVENESS

"I balance" | *"I sense"*

Air, Venus, Cardinal | *Negative Fire, Yang*

Magnetism personified. The Libra born in a Snake year will, above all, attract. This combination is a mostly happy one. People born under this sign may be less so. This is because they are not only irresistible; they are also stubborn and willful. They want things done their way, and like to order others around subtly. Often, things are done for them, their way, by willing lackeys. These people have charisma to burn.

Libran Snakes rule others through emotion. They are capable of sensing exactly what another needs from them. They are remarkably perceptive and even have a gift for the supernatural. Librans born in Snake years know how to exalt an audience with their cool, reasonable yet emphatically sentimental discourse. These people are born to serve as shepherds of human flocks, moralizers and brotherhood mongers.

There is a Saint Valentine quality about the Libra born Snake person. A lacy, heart- shaped, whimsical yet meaningful self that always shines through. I'd say that this sign is more "feminine" than masculine in flavor. Libra/Snakes indulge in finery. They like to "mother" others. And they embody a kind of exemplary passivity that lends a quality of femaleness to their characters. They are not wont to go after power over their fellows unless it is requested of them by followers. In fact, Libra/Snakes have to contend with laziness, luxuriating, dissipation and wanton pleasure-seeking. They are given to excess and must do everyday battle with a monumental delight in languor.

Their fatal flaw in all of this is, of course, their inability to escape their own seductiveness. Eventually, after years of watching people fall at his or her feet in admiration, the Libra/Snake gets the picture and usually becomes a pacesetter of some sort. Taking up causes is, in the case of Libran Snakes, always performed in the most graceful and non-violent way. Libra/Snake wants to reason with danger, to talk over differences, to discuss the peace arrangements. Then he will make a touching speech on the subject, and more people will collapse at his feet. Libra/Snake doesn't have to overpower. All he has to do is attract.

One quality that the Libra/Snake possesses and frequently uses in his or her profession is humanitarianism. The Libra side of this person's character wants justice for all. The Snake is kindness itself, always compassionate and understanding, willing to lend an ear or a shoulder to cry on. The two signs together create a being of enormous altruism, who is not afraid to do something about hunger or poverty or injustice. The rosters of international relief organizations are loaded with the names of Libra/Snakes who care about their fellow man enough to spend their time and money to help out.

Not that the Libra/Snake is basically generous. He is not. This person might even be slightly guarded about spending money on necessities. Yet, when he feels the urge, he indulges in an expensive bibelot or adorns himself with some golden gadgetry or other. Libra/Snake is a sneaky spender and is not above a fib or two about how much baubles really cost.

Love

Does the Libra/Snake know anything else? These subjects are all love and sensuality, sexiness and grand romance. Of course, they are too gorgeous to be forever faithful to one person. But they are definitely devoted mates in every other way. Too, Libra/Snakes, for all of their beauty and languor, can be a lot of fun. They are mischievous, a little zany, and they know how to laugh at themselves.

If you are attracted to one of these miracles of charm, I suggest you adopt his or her ideals immediately. You will be needing all the patience and pacifism you can get when your Libra/Snake goes off on a tour of African hunger areas without you, leaving you home to keep the kids alive. You will need great personal fortitude and lots of dignity to walk beside your beloved Libra/Snake. Keep your nose in the air and don't give that adoring crowd the time of day.

Compatibilities

Roosters are high on your priority list. Try sticking to those Roosters born in Gemini, Leo, Sagittarius and Aquarius. Leo, Sagittarius and Aquarius/Oxen make swell bedfellows for you too. Aries and Capricorn/Monkeys get on your nerves. Cancer and Capricorn/Pigs are too critically scrupulous for your slightly slippery attitudes to jibe with theirs. And Cancer/Tigers are so moody and jumpy as to drive you up a wall.

Home and Family

Count on the Libra born in Snake years to furnish his or her environment in plush fabrics and line the walls with precious objets d'art. This person is a lover of luxury and, despite his sackcloth and ashes pitch, adores comforts and hates to live without them. You will be welcome at the Libra/Snake's home, too. Feel free to drop in any time. There's always enough room for a few more uninvited guests.

The Libra/Snake will want to have lots of children. This character enjoys caretaking and protecting others. He or she may, for this reason, mollycoddle a bit too much and hover anxiously over his sleeping bambinos. But when they awaken they will be in for a good time. Libra/Snake parents bedazzle their kids the same way they enchant everyone else. However, these parents tend to preach. Their sermonizing must be quelled. Moralizing sets kids' teeth on edge.

As a child this person will be delightfully winning and have a kind of funny grownup wisdom in speech. Too much material spoiling is not good for this sensitive child. He or she must be taught the value of basics. Nature hikes and camping trips will remove some of that city glitter from his eyes. I highly recommend sports and scouts. This child can be subject to psychosomatic allergies if he or she is not regularly brought firmly to earth by routine and security.

Profession

By nature, the Libra/Snake is a leader of men. But he or she is non-competitive and wants no part of belligerence. The gift here is attractiveness. People willingly revere this subject, hang on his every word and long to be like him or her. Misused, this talent can, of course, be extremely dangerous. But as the Libra/Snake is not so power-hungry as he is willing to take the reins if they are given him, there is less danger here than may be feared.

The Libra/Snake does not take well to subordination. It's not that he or she cannot understand the need for humility, but that the underling station annoys them. They know they can run the show, so they wonder why somebody doesn't just hang a sign on their door saying "Boss." But they don't misuse power as a rule, and are as conscientious as those who work with them. Libra/Snakes make excellent partners for less charismatic people who know how to do earthly things like add and subtract and pay their taxes. Libra/Snakes want top billing but don't rankle at sharing the profits.

Some good career choices for the Libra/Snake are: spiritual leader, model, actor, singer, talk show host, executive officer, newscaster, politician.

Famous Libra/Snakes: Mahatma Gandhi, Thelonious Monk, Jesse Jackson, Alfred Nobel, Anne Rice, Chubby Checker, Linda McCartney, Paul Simon, Pierre Bellemare.

The New Astrology

LIBRA	HORSE

JUSTICE	QUARRELSOMENESS	PERSUASIVENESS	SELFISHNESS
AESTHETICS	MANIPULATION	UNSCRUPULOUSNESS	AUTONOMY
CHARM	PROCRASTINATION	POPULARITY	REBELLION
GENTILITY	SELF-INDULGENCE	STYLE	HASTE
EQUILIBRIUM	INDECISION	DEXTERITY	ANXIETY
IDEALISM	TALKATIVENESS	ACCOMPLISHMENT	PRAGMATISM

"I balance"   *"I demand"*

Air, Venus, Cardinal   *Positive Fire, Yang*

For a Horse character this person born in gracious Libra will be genteel and dignified. Horses are sometimes rebellious and hardheaded. Libra practically never is. Libra wants peace and knows how to go after equilibrium. In this sign, Libra climbs on to the Horse's back and hangs on for dear life until she has tamed the selfish stallion into a better, more civilized person.

When joined to Libra, the Horse personality gets to keep many of his worldly goods. He retains full interest in his elegance and style. He hangs on tight to popularity and has the market cornered on idealism. Libra lends Horse refined taste. Moreover, in hitching his wagon to Libra, the Horse doesn't have to give up one iota of his fancy. You know how Horses only like to do what they want when they want to? Well, Libra doesn't mind that. In fact, Libra encourages this quality, as she knows that with her well-developed sense of measure the Horse will never totally buck the system.

This blend of signs often hatches excellent talkers. The Horse has a commanding presence. He or she will captivate audiences with poise and self-assuredness. Libra adds charm and a touch of the aesthetic to this popular image. The Libra born Horse can be an impressive performer.

Horses born in Libra often experience the phenomenon of unusual destiny. This obviously has to do with their gift for being in the right place at the right time. The Libra/Horse is very mobile and is concerned with self-advancement. The combination of good luck and a nose for connections makes this person a fine candidate for sudden, unexpected fame or fortune.

No Horse character is ever lazy. But Libran Horses will be slightly less hectic than their counterparts in other signs. They know how to relax and slow down for the sake of gain or improvement and are not so preoccupied with the pragmatic as most Horses. The Libra/Horse is an exalted type of person, whose opinions and stances are fiery and willful. You will not forget meeting up with one. And, as they are extremely sociable, you may very well encounter one at a party this very evening. Parties and gatherings, receptions and meetings play a large role in this person's life.

The Libra/Horse is, above all, a convincing person. He is persuasive and eloquent. He is not very compassionate or sentimental. But he can be carried away by the fervor of an ideal. There is poetry in the soul of this effective human being and it shows on his dignified, tasteful surface. He can be unscrupulous for self-interest's sake, and if he's trying to talk you into one of his plans he will never take no for an answer.

The Horse born in Libra seeks justice for all and favor for himself. He usually achieves autonomy and is not above creating a scandal to get it. The Libra/Horse is an oddball, and often invents or performs some outrageous deed to shock more conventional souls. But never mind. This person does not suffer from self-doubt, but goes straight for the jugular—ever so elegantly.

Love

Passion is more important than tenderness in the life of a Libra/Horse. He or she will be attracted by ideals in another person, or by some characteristic besides appearance—like money, for example. Libra/Horses are not quite so rapacious as most Libras, but they nonetheless like to take a room by storm. They are sensuous and given to flirting.

Loving someone born in Libra/Horse can present complications. This person is something of an island unto him- or herself. They are not too dependent on the image of a relationship and will seek in a partner the capacity for self-sacrifice that Libra/Horse lacks. If you love one of these creatures, get ready to spend a good part of your time combing that luxuriant mane and rubbing down your beautiful steed. The Libra/Horse is a primper and a preener.

Compatibilities

Seek a life partner from among Tiger people born in Gemini, Leo, Sagittarius or Aquarius. Flings can turn into much more when dabbled in with either a Gemini or a Leo/Goat. Sagittarius and Aquarius/Dogs make earnest companions for you. I don't advise you to dally with Rats born in Aries, Cancer or Capricorn. Discourage passes from eager Capricorn/Goats too.

Home and Family

Here the Libra/Horse will really go for broke. This native wants a handsome home atmosphere where he or she can receive platoons of friends and associates. The sofas will be velvet and the drapes heavy and probably burgundy or soft brown. Libra/Horse is a luxury-lover extraordinaire. He will also be sure to own every last device to enhance the household's appearance. The lights will all be on dimmer switches and the flowers freshly arranged by the person who comes in for just that purpose. Libra/Horse spares no expense when it comes to impressing his audience. He deplores vulgarity and does not take kindly to guests who show up in tattered blue jeans. Flair's the thing.

There will be a distance between this character and his or her offspring. The Horse born in Libra may feel some competition from children. He or she will require help in raising kids as the Libra/Horse is frequently out or too busy doing something personal to care for them. Actually I think the average Libra/Horse gets on best with his or her kids when the kids start being grownups. Then, when the petulant childishness has begun to fade, the child will become more acceptable to the tasteful Libra/Horse.

As a child this person will show great promise and impress adults with his apparent ease in acquiring social graces. There is rebelliousness in the young Libran born Horse that wanes when the child matures and sees that tempestuousness will not get her where she wants to go. This kid can be funny and quirky—a sort of odd man out with his cronies. Yet the Libra/Horse will always be well liked and admired. No matter what you do as his parent, this child will eventually go his own way.

Profession

As this person is both argumentative and persuasive, he or she will excel at all jobs requiring verbal skill and conviction. Moreover, the Libra/Horse is elegantly well dressed and presents a fine image to the world. His or her weakness will stem from an unwillingness to play the game for the sake of keeping the peace. Libra/Horses care less about peace than they do about their own advancement. They will only be cooperative if compromise in no way impedes their progress.

Depending on the situation, this person can either shine at dispensing authority or at taking orders. The only prerequisite, as far as the Libra/Horse is concerned, is personal interest. If being the boss gets Libra/Horse to the top, then he'll gladly accept an executive post. Otherwise, you can keep your lofty titles. All the Libra/Horse really wants from a job is upward mobility- and, of course, money.

Careers accessible to Libran Horses are: city planner, landscape architect, gossip columnist, critic, merchant, publicist, actor, restaurant owner, decorator, teacher.

Some famous Libra/Horses: Dmitri Shostakovitch, Rita Hayworth, Penny Marshall, Eric Charden, Hafiz al-Assade (Syria), Harold Pinter, Jimmy Breslin, Jonathan Lipnicki, Leopold Senghor, Luke Perry, Philippe Noiret, Rutherford B. Hayes.

The New Astrology

LIBRA		GOAT	

JUSTICE	QUARRELSOMENESS	INVENTION	PARASITISM
AESTHETICS	MANIPULATION	LACK OF FORESIGHT	SENSITIVITY
CHARM	PROCRASTINATION	PERSEVERANCE	TARDINESS
GENTILITY	SELF-INDULGENCE	WHIMSY	PESSIMISM
EQUILIBRIUM	INDECISION	GOOD MANNERS	TASTE
IDEALISM	TALKATIVENESS	IMPRACTICALITY	WORRY
"I balance"		*"I depend"*	
Air, Venus, Cardinal		*Negative Fire, Yang*	

Ostensibly a dependent lover of beauty and equilibrium, this person claims to need a peaceful environment, but we know better. Librans born in Goat years are testy and quarrelsome people. They love an argument, a good old heated discussion, a challenge. The Libra/Goat requires the regard of his peers. He likes to be looked at, contemplated, taken seriously and admired. To this end, the Libra/Goat will do almost anything—once.

With Libra and Goat under the same roof, people born in this sign will be doubly attracted to elegance and finesse. They truly prefer to furnish their lives with ornate classics and line their walls with books than to spend time and money on trendy wardrobes or spiffy automobiles. These characters can be social climbers. As such, they prefer to climb culturally rather than merely be included in the annals of society, party-giving or going. Libra/Goats are a bit light-headed. But they are not superficial.

There is great creativity in the Libra/Goat nature. This person, provided the ambience is secure and safe, can invent and imagine all manner of craft and artisanry. I would not say this subject is a gifted artist in the Picasso sense. But there is, inside the Libra/Goat head, a kaleidoscopic imagination.

The Libra/Goat leaps from idea to idea with a special rapid grace all his own. He understands the labyrinthine. He comprehends complexity, and is superbly talented at all sorts of communication.

One of the Goat/Libra's handicaps is his unwillingness to believe in self. I say unwillingness rather than inability because the phenomenon is more a refusal than a lack. "I can't. Who cares? Who wants to listen to little old me? It's not really important. Never mind." That's the kind of talk you hear from non-directed Librans born in Goat years.

You see, Librans born in Goat years are extremely sensitive. In their youth they are often drawn to strong, stable types whose very presence seems to promise to shore up their courage. Then, after a while, when the weirdo Libra/Goat sees just what a high price he must pay to be "normal" and "stable," when he grasps the useless, boring sameness of a life without creation or experiment, he bolts. But this bolting seems to Libra/Goat a terribly cowardly act. He is disappointed in normalcy. But he blames his disappointment on his own unwillingness to "go straight." This, once again, makes him lose confidence in himself. As he never had masses of self-belief in the first place, this makes him less effective, and a vicious circle effect sets in.

Libra/Goats are excessive. They are vulnerable to addiction. They are ambitious and fashion-conscious. They are inventive and talented in all sorts of glamour-related pursuits. The trouble with Libra/Goats, besides their intermittent lack of self-assurance, is that they tend to disperse their energies in too many flittings about. They are easily distracted. They must learn to settle on one idea and push it through to its logical conclusion. And they must seek the wisdom of those more thoughtful and sagacious than they. It is by heeding good advice and not flying off the handle till the wood is all chopped that Librans born in Goat years will succeed.

Love

Romance is one area in which the Libra/Goat feels comfortable and capable. This person is gifted for sentimental rapport. He or she will revel in the trappings of love: the candlelight dinners and the trips to tropical islands, the banter and, of course, the sex. Libra/Goats are very pretty people, sort of frail looking and fey. They always dress to suit their looks and have a finely developed nose for style. They will depend entirely on their relationships with their mates. Living alone is out of the question. These people thrive on tenderness and offer top drawer companionship to a mate.

If you love a Libra/Goat, you must first win his or her favors through clever and aesthetic courtship methods. Your Libra born Goat is fatally attractive. You will not be the only one seeking his or her affections. Be unusual. The Libra/Goat cleaves to the arcane and is fascinated by the strange. Ordinary workaday people only attract the Libra/Goat in his very first blush of youthful naiveté.

Compatibilities

You have a propensity for cohabitation with Cat people. You'll want to choose from Cats born in Gemini, Leo, Sagittarius and Aquarius. There are plenty of Horse subjects out there for your pleasure, too. Try sticking to Gemini, Sagittarius or Aquarius/Horses. They have the necessary earning power to keep you in style. Leo and Aquarius/Pigs also enjoy high standards of living. Aries, Cancer and Capricorn/Dogs are out of the running, as are Cancer and Capricorn/Oxen.

Home and Family

The Libra/Goat is not terribly concerned with decoration. He will be happiest in a messy, intellectual sort of decor with deep worn velvet or leather armchairs and generous working surfaces. He's not overly conscious of how his or her interior strikes others. He wants it to be comfortable first and beautiful later. Libra/Goats enjoy the haphazardness of the "lived-in" look.

These people make conscientious parents who want the best in culture for their children. Occasionally Libra/Goats seem to be overwhelmed by their children and even a bit bamboozled by them. They don't like to discipline their kids. But neither can they tolerate being a punching bag for little Johnny or Mary. Often, they allow trouble to build up before stepping in to do something about it. This avant-garde childrearing method leads to its share of yelling.

Libra/Goat kids are too sweet for words. They are loving and enchanting little people whose beauty alone is enough to make you want to squeeze them. My advice? Don't. Libra/Goat children, like their adult counterparts, are not as fragile as they look. They hate to be treated like dumbbells. These bright people gobble education. The best schools are in order.

Profession

Libra/Goats are not independent people. They must be surrounded by aides-de-camp or buoyed by a well-constructed system in order to achieve their goals. They are talented and innovative. Libra/Goats have natural poise and are mannerly and dress tastefully. They are especially gifted for complex creative work requiring a sense of true invention. Libra/Goats are easily discouraged and can very quickly be overcome by the prospect of having too much on their plates. One dish at a time is the method best suited to the advancement of their artistic natures.

Jobs that best suit Libra/Goats are: freelance illustrator, poet, fashion journalist, scriptwriter, homemaker, graphic artist, musician.

Famous Libra/Goats: Franz Liszt, Pierre Trudeau, John Le Carré, Doris Lessing, Chevy Chase, Barbara Walters, Yo-Yo Ma, Catherine Deneuve, Anita Ekberg, Anthony Newley, Desmond Tutu, Lech Walesa, Julez Roy, Julio Iglesias, Mickey Mantle, Miguel de Cervantes, Pierre Trudeau.

The New Astrology

LIBRA

JUSTICE	QUARRELSOMENESS
AESTHETICS	MANIPULATION
CHARM	PROCRASTINATION
GENTILITY	SELF-INDULGENCE
EQUILIBRIUM	INDECISION
IDEALISM	TALKATIVENESS

"I balance"

Air, Venus, Cardinal

MONKEY

IMPROVISATION	DECEIT
CUNNING	RUSE
STABILITY	LOQUACITY
SELF-INVOLVEMENT	LEADERS
WIT	SILLINESS
OPPORTUNISM	ZEAL

"I plan"

Positive Metal, Yin

This combination of signs can talk his or her way in or out of just about any paper bag. The Libra/Monkey's strength lies in his brilliant manipulation of words and ideas to fit situations both commercial and artistic. Librans born Monkey are gentle con artists whose characteristic eloquence and gift of gab make them thrilling company.

The Libra side of this person's nature will want to live life as a couple and will be attracted to early marriage. Adding Monkey traits to the jabbery Libra's chart infuses it with an increased need for communication—and even a certain desire for healthy conflict. The Libra/Monkey combo is not restful. These people are attracted to motion for its own sake. Sometimes they need to forget what they have just seen and travel on to new territories in order to soak up some joyful or at least different vibrations.

The Libra born Monkey is manipulative. He or she will not be above exploitation of others. The Libra/Monkey sees the world as his playpen. He doesn't see why he should not extract sentiment in favor of gain. After all, whatever shenanigans the Monkey born Libra is up to, he will be the first to assure both you and himself that he has the best interests of everyone concerned at heart. Libra/Monkey is not a parasite. He is active and energetic, has sharper than average intelligence and can be wittily clever.

There is a freewheeling aspect to the Libra/Monkey personality. This person exudes boyishness and carries a twinkle around in his eye that intimates that he has caught his entire entourage with their hands in the cookie jar. Libran Monkeys don't go around policing the world. They are intuitive and feel both personal and social changes very strongly. Often, you will find Libra/Monkeys in the vanguard of an artistic or political movement.

Life is sometimes just too much for the Libra/Monkey's heightened sensitivities to bear. This character can be drawn to inducing euphoria and ingesting consciousness-altering substances. He doesn't always feel strong enough, combative enough—although he is obviously smart enough, by a long shot—to meet a challenge.

Not that Libra/Monkeys are weak. Far from it! But they can lack self-assurance and hesitate before steamrolling a competitor. They don't mind winning through guile or shiftiness. But they really prefer not to confront adversity head on. Might, where the Libra/Monkey is concerned, is never right. He prefers satire as a weapon. He'd rather use humor or even just his brains to outdistance opposition. The Libra/Monkey is skilled at dealing with his audience. He has dignity and a biting repartee. His talents are many and he can rise to great heights in any area he chooses because of his willingness to adapt, to bend and change with the current. This person is the antithesis of stubborn. Although he can be discouraged and may indulge in temporary surrender, the Libra/Monkey is flexible and even-tempered.

Love

In romantic endeavors as in more prosaic pursuits, the Libra born Monkey can be deceptively self-interested. Mostly, though, as the couple is of paramount importance in this person's life, the interests of maintaining that relationship will take precedence over all others. Libra/Monkeys are sentimental, and even when they take unfair advantage of another's love for them, they remain devotedly attached. What Libra/Monkeys are looking for in love affairs or marriages is a balance between two people whose mutual passion and interdependency can create a symbiosis. As Libra/Monkey takes, so he or she will give in return.

Should you be enamored of a Libra/Monkey, you can rest assured he or she will make of your rapport an idealistic mission in search of lifelong equilibrium. Their hopes are so high, in fact, that it can put quite a bit of wearying responsibility on their better halves. The Libra/Monkey wants to be the stable element in your couple, which will give you the chance to go ahead and be about as loony as you like. Don't worry, Libra/Monkey will provide emotionally.

Compatibilities

There might be a Dragon in your future. If so, he or she will best be chosen from among Gemini, Leo, Sagittarius or Aquarius subjects. You will also get on with Leo, Sagittarius and Aquarius/Rats. The vibes are not perfect between you and Aries or Cancer/Horses. Ditto for Cancer or Capricorn/Tigers. Cancer/Pigs and Capricorn/Oxen are just plain too rigid for your lithe and changeable nature to enjoy for long.

Home and Family

The Libra/Monkey's home is where he hangs his hat. He likes beauty and luxury but doesn't necessarily need a mammoth homestead to prove to himself that he has roots. Libra/Monkeys are rooted in the moment. It seems to be enough for them. They are not nomads or hobos. But if they do have a lovely home, its purpose will more likely be to please others than to lend security.

The Libra/Monkey makes a sincere and loving parent. One thing he or she regrets in the first place is having had to grow up and become serious and stodgy and adult. So this person will be the kind who plays with kids, and takes them to amusement parks, and accompanies them on roller coaster rides. Libra/Monkeys will expect their children to be imaginative and encourage them in creative areas.

Libra/Monkey kids are sweet little things. They have a ready smile and are always willing to go along with Auntie Linda or leap into the unsuspecting arms of Uncle Oscar. They are both gregarious and sunny. Of course, they must be watched for naughtiness. These kids are mischief-makers of the first water. They are always up to something. Also, they tend to jabber your ear off. Give them lots of good education so at least when they grow up they'll have something interesting to jabber about.

Profession

The Monkey born Libra boasts an aristocratic bearing. We know by now that he or she also possesses the ability to talk—at length. There is, as well, a talent for adapting words to ideas. The Libran Monkey makes an excellent colleague or partner, and handles exterior relations better than any other Monkey signs. The Libra/Monkey boss figure will not be terrifying at all, but rather will impress by his loquacity and razor-sharp mind. People respect the Libran/Monkey for his noble touch and acuity about world affairs or social developments.

Profitable ways to employ the Libra/Monkey's services: Either leave him or her entirely alone in a windowless room, thereby enforcing concentration, or send him or her on the road selling—anything! But make sure they meet their daily quota. Libra/Monkeys have a sorry tendency to disperse their energies in vapid chitchat.

Any career is suitable for Libra/Monkey if it guarantees movement and social contact: realtor, actor, professor, insurance salesman, speechwriter, legal aide, social worker, public relations, advertising "idea" person.

Famous Libra/Monkeys: Buster Keaton, F. Scott Fitzgerald, Jacques Tati, John Kenneth Galbraith, Timothy Leary, Ashanti, Diane Dufresne, Eleanor Roosevelt, F. Scott Fitzgerald, Glenn Gould, Henri de Verneuil, Hugh Jackman, Jacques Sallebert, Mario Puzo, Martina Hingis, Martina Navratilova, Montgomerey Clift, Ray Charles, Walter Matthau, William Conrad.

The New Astrology

LIBRA

JUSTICE	QUARRELSOMENESS
AESTHETICS	MANIPULATION
CHARM	PROCRASTINATION
GENTILITY	SELF-INDULGENCE
EQUILIBRIUM	INDECISION
IDEALISM	TALKATIVENESS

"I balance"

Air, Venus, Cardinal

ROOSTER

RESILIENCE	COCKINESS
ENTHUSIASM	BOASTFULNESS
CANDOR	BLIND FAITH
CONSERVATISM	PEDANTRY
CHIC	BOSSINESS
HUMOR	DISSIPATION

"I overcome"

Negative Metal, Yang

Libra/Rooster lives a life full of chasms of despair followed by summits of felicity. And thank Zeus for Libra's sense of equilibrium. Libra lends poetry to the Rooster's cocky strictness and tickles his conservatism, even prodding it into the occasional flight of fancy. Also, Libra tempers the Rooster's tendency to overreact. For a Rooster, this person will be gentle and might even qualify as "calm."

What does Rooster, then, give to our friend Libra in exchange? Plenty. For one, Rooster's earthiness and enthusiasm lift the lid off Libra's occasional self-indulgence. "Come on now, Libra old girl, you've got to work. You cannot just lie there in your satin sheets reading confession magazines. Up and at 'em. There's a new toy out in the kitchen, a fascinating event on the front porch, a terrific person to meet on the sidewalk," urges the eager Rooster. Rooster's resilience plays an interesting role in the Libra/Rooster personality. As we already know, Libra does not take stands. He or she is not hastily judgmental. The Rooster's life is constantly being saved at the last minute by his innate ability to accept and undergo upheaval that would kill anyone less bouncy. These two qualities are highly complementary and give Libra/Rooster an edge when it comes to some of the sharper turns on the highway of life. Rooster knows how to brush off the experience without a blink, and Libra doesn't judge him for having done so. This person has few, if any, regrets.

Rooster brings rigor and energy to the Libra subject and his candor lightens Libra's sometimes unnecessarily feisty speech. To Rooster, Libra lends an air of relaxed attractiveness often missing from the bossy and cocky Rooster image. Libra/Rooster is mild-mannered, tweedily clad, and appears to have no axe to grind. The image is appealing. Roosters born in Libra are popular with peers. There is something of the quiet know- it-all here. The smarty pants attitude.

This person can be accused of self-complacency. The impression is: "I'm right because I'm me." It can be a bore. This Rooster does not exhaust himself at workaday jobs.. He likes to shine, be brilliant and knock 'em dead in a single performance. Reruns don't interest the Libra/Rooster. He'd rather you would suggest a new endeavor or ask him to perform one of his works in progress. This person is a hive of novelty. He does not lack for surprises.

All in all, this Rooster is talented and sensitive enough to create both poetry and music. He or she can take artistic careers far. They have stick-to-itiveness and they can present their material in a winning (Libran) manner. They are slightly conflictual and seem to take pleasure in philosophical tugs of war. It's just as well; it gets the job done.

Love

The Libra/Rooster wants to respect as well as love his or partner. He has enormous devotion and faith to offer. But he does not want to give it away foolishly. Rooster usually settles on one love object and is able to maintain interest in a single mate for life. Not all Roosters are so lucky. But the Libra side of this one gives him extra sensitivity.

If you love one of these Librans, you must be very happy. Libra/Rooster is a person you can look up to, admire and feel sweet about as well. Libra/Roosters appreciate tenderness and know how to receive affection. They may seem a bit preoccupied with their eternal artistic flights of fancy. Don't worry. If they said they loved you, they mean it. If not, you'd better look elsewhere. This person is unbudgeable in the fidelity department.

Compatibilities

I see you happiest with an Ox or Snake character. The atmosphere will be best if you take care to select your partners from Oxen and Snakes born in Gemini, Leo, Sagittarius or Aquarius. Discriminate. Don't be too tempted by Aries/Pigs, Cancer/Roosters and Capricorn/Cats. Each in his or her own way is too emotionally unstable to give you what you really need—coolheadedness and tranquility.

Home and Family

The Libra/Rooster does not wish to show off with his posh decorating scheme. This person is an outside man or woman. He likes his place of habitation to be well appointed, but he doesn't want to pound the nails or sew up the curtains himself. Libra/Rooster feels a closer involvement in his or her cerebral work than in any manual labor, no matter how lofty. If the house is practical and traditionally furnished, Libra/Rooster will be content with it.

This person's parenting talents will be limited to guidance and a rather distant sort of sunny affection. Libra/Roosters do not wish to wipe bottoms. They'd rather hire a nanny. Libra/Roosters are not exactly family types anyway. They enjoy being part of a couple. But they don't really have time for running the PTA or selling cookies for the Girl Scouts.

The Libra/Rooster child will be active and loving. He or she needs much cultural input at a young age. The fine sensitivity of this child will want stimulating. Nature and all of its joys have a calming effect on the Libra/Rooster child. He will be an odd mix of activity and repose. No matter how you parent this kid, he'll be okay. But the more attention you pay to his intellectual development the better.

Profession

Gifted in all things poetic, this person has a real chance to apply his artistic skills in life and to achieve public acclaim. Normally Libra turns away from the natural conflicts that haunt the shadows of notoriety. But here, Rooster comes along and struts through the curtain to sing you a little song while you are figuring out the complexities of a contract. Libra coupled with Rooster is a combination almost destined for some degree of fame. This is not your everyday run-of-the-mill human being.

In order to utilize Libra/Rooster's capacity for artistic endeavor, he or she must (and almost always does) begin work at a young age. He can try to fit into some system or even invent his own. But within either of these he must feel he's being treated with deference. If the Libra/Rooster's opinions are not heard, he is not pleased. You might think he'd make a good boss. But I think, paradoxically, that he'd rather not have to direct anyone. He really wants to be free, to create, to react, to invent, to expound.

Libra/Roosters make resigned employees. They understand the need for working at a paying job. But they'd really rather not. They want to be active. On their own terms.

Some good career choices for the Libra/Rooster might be: naturalist, singer, poet, screenwriter, TV producer, photographer, critic.

Some famous Libra/Roosters: Giuseppe Verdi, Louis Aragon, William Faulkner, Al Capp, Yves Montand, Catherine Zeta Jones, Charles Merrill, Deborah Kerr, Geneviève Dorman, Georges Brassens, James Whitmore, Jesse Helms, Jim McKay, Louis Aragon, Serena Williams, Tom Poston, Yves Montand, Zachery Bryan.

The New Astrology

LIBRA	DOG

JUSTICE	QUARRELSOMENESS	CONSTANCY	UNEASINES
AESTHETICS	MANIPULATION	UNSOCIABILITY	CRITICISM
CHARM	PROCRASTINATION	RESPECTABILITY	DUTY
GENTILITY	SELF-INDULGENCE	SELF-RIGHTEOUSNESS	CYNICISM
EQUILIBRIUM	INDECISION	INTELLIGENCE	HEROISM
IDEALISM	TALKATIVENESS	TACTLESSNESS	MORALITY

"I balance"   *"I worry"*

Air, Venus, Cardinal   *Positive Metal, Yang*

An altruist. A worrywart. An idealist. A complainer. An aesthete. A scientist. A handyman. A bon vivant. Need I say more? Of course I must. I have a book to write here.

Libra/Dogs are dignified and brilliant. They possess innate humanitarianism and are soft-hearted in the best possible way. You will always be able to get sympathy from a Libra/Dog. He will help you, cheer you along and applaud your courage. He's a great friend, a super associate and a bundle of nerves. Libra is able to sort out any of life's conflicts through diplomacy and impartiality. In fact, one of the most annoying things about Libras is their refusal to take unpopular stands. They can always see both sides.

Dogs are not unlike this. They don't favor conflict unless it's absolutely unavoidable self-defense. So when you put the two signs together you get a very pacific and merciful creature who wouldn't hurt a flea—unless, of course, he feels personally threatened. When that happens, get out the muzzle!

Libra/Dogs gripe a lot. They complain about how bad life is and how many evil bounders are wallowing about in the world stealing from poor people and hurting the handicapped. They carp and they are wont to snap as well. Of course their bark is ever so much worse than their bite. But nonetheless, life with Libra/Dog can be trying.

Librans born in Dog years always try to settle differences through compromise. They understand that you don't want to eat your soup because you hate onions. There are plenty of reasons to hate onions, heaven knows. When I was a child I didn't exactly love onions myself. And it's true that my mother forced me to eat them. I sure didn't like that. So I can see how you would hesitate. Where you or I might say, "Eat your damned soup and be glad you have something to eat!," inspiring tears and even indigestion, Libra/Dog will trot all around the issue in such a compassionate way that it'll be Thursday by the time his victim eats his soup.

Of course Libra/Dogs get walked all over by unscrupulous blackguards. They take unheard-of flak from family and friends who never hesitate to use and abuse their hospitality and services. They are just too darned nice. They know it. They feel it. Then, when they are up to their necks in sycophants and hangers-on, they start to bitch. But by this time nobody can hear the Libra/Dog's complaints. By now everyone is so used to his self-sacrificing act that his pleas for help fall on deaf ears.

Does he gain circumspection by this means? Not on your life he doesn't. The Libra/Dog always sticks to his beliefs and adheres to his causes with a fervor and zeal like nobody else's. No matter how tense the family holidays were last year, she will always say, "Of course you can come for Christmas. Bring the kids."

Libra/Dogs are dexterous with their hands. They make models and build furniture, draw up charts and know how to grow things. They are kindly and home-loving. But they can be snappish and dry, hesitant and moody, too.

Love

Libra/Dogs are choosy about their love partners. As much as they don't mind peopling their social life with ne'er-do-wells and unfortunates, Librans born in Dog years take meticulous care not to choose an unworthy partner. They are gifted in love relationships, but they are also afraid of excessive intimacy. They don't like to take criticism as much as they like to dish it out. Cohabitation is not their forte.

If you love a Libra/Dog, be patient. Learn how to wait (years!) for him or her to make a decision about settling down. Show how helpful you can be and agree with all of Libra/Dog's humanitarian schemes. Don't be afraid to leave him or her alone. Libra/Dogs know very well how to amuse themselves by puttering. Don't cling. Wait.

Compatibilities

Be wary and settle on a magnanimously magnetic yet understanding Tiger. Choose him or her from among those born in Gemini, Sagittarius or Aquarius. You can get on well with Cats born in Gemini, Leo or Aquarius, too. And you will blend in perfectly with the exciting lifestyles of Leo and Sagittarius/Horses. Gemini/Snakes are cute, too. And you will admire their cheerful incisiveness. Dragons are most definitely out, especially if they were born in Aries, Cancer or Capricorn. You don't have much affinity for Cancer or Capricorn/Goats. A Cancer born in a Monkey year will get on your already testy nerves.

Home and Family

The Libra/Dog will be happiest in the country. The city and its harshness grate on his delicate nervous system. The interior of his home will be neat and orderly. His tastes will run to the slick and modern. Yet his favorite colors will be earthy reds and yellows.

The Libra/Dog parent is self-sacrificial. But then Libra/Dogs usually marry late (if at all) and seldom have children. They are loving and kind to their kids if they do have them. But they are also very critical and can be sarcastic. They know how to provide for their kids and they like the cozy atmosphere of family life.

Little Libra/Dogs will be charmers. Everybody in the whole neighborhood will like this tot. He or she will be smiley and outgoing, sincere and a mite outspoken. Don't put early achievements past this little Libra/Dog. This kid may be tops in his nursery school class and stay up there for his whole career. Duty and responsibility come early to this character. Tickle him or her for at least one minute a day.

Profession

Members of this sign are talented in jobs that require technical skill, human understanding or the chance to please their fellow man. Libra/Dogs like nature and animals. They care about social order, and are interested in politics and the law. This person is a bit of a poet, too. His force is his kindness. His weakness is his kindness, too.

People like their Libra/Dog bosses. There is always a spirit of democracy and camaraderie around the office when a Libra/Dog is running the show. Also, employees respect this person's humane notions and will work hard to come up to the Libra/Dog's high standards. It's easy for the Libra/Dog to be an employee. He is never a person with something to prove or with a mission to get ahead of others or beat out the competition. He or she just wants a pleasant, safe and sane existence.

Libra/Dogs are capable of lifelong routine jobs as a means to the ideal they are always searching for in their private lives. Some careers that will suit this character are: veterinarian, social worker, doctor, midwife, animal trainer, landscape gardener, research scientist, Internet wizard.

Famous Libra/Dogs: Charles Ives, George Gershwin, Brigitte Bardot, Amy Jo Johnson, David Ben-Gurion, John Wooden, Kelly Ripa, Kirk Cameron, Matt Damon, Nana Mouscouri, Susan Sarandon.

The New Astrology

LIBRA	PIG

JUSTICE	QUARRELSOMENESS	SCRUPULOUSNESS	CREDULITY
AESTHETICS	MANIPULATION	GALLANTRY	WRATH
CHARM	PROCRASTINATION	SINCERITY	HESITATION
GENTILITY	SELF-INDULGENCE	VOLUPTUOUSNESS	MATERIALISM
EQUILIBRIUM	INDECISION	CULTURE	GOURMANDISM
IDEALISM	TALKATIVENESS	HONESTY	PIGHEADEDNESS

"I balance"

Air, Venus, Cardinal

"I civilize"

Negative Water, Yin

Loving is what the Libra/Pig does best. This person is devoted, exclusive, jealous and loyal to a fault. Nothing really counts much in the Libran Pig's life except the relationship he or she has with a mate. All activity centers around the bond that Libra/Pig has created with someone else. Householding, money, children, hobbies, friendships—you name it—will be relegated to second place. The marriage (or love affair) is the sun. It governs every gesture, every effort, and every joy and sorrow.

Libra requires loveliness in order to survive. Pigs need riches. Libra is able to create her own beauty and longs to be free to admire it in a peaceful ambiance. Pigs also enjoy peaceful surroundings. They are enslaved to cultural pursuits of all manner and variety. They thrive on opulence. If the Libra/Pig has his "druthers," he'll live comfortably ensconced in a luxurious love affair for all of his days.

The Libra/Pig's goal, although it may not always appear so, is to feel spoiled. This person languishes in dreams of magnificence and glut. She may secretly wish she were a movie star or at least a fairy princess or a queen. The mundane workaday routine at which Libra/Pig excels is but a secret stepping stone to that place where, when his ship comes in, all squalor and discord will be transformed into gaiety and charm, enjoyment, excess, gentility and voluptuousness. People in the Libra/Pig's dream world will anoint him with oils and tender him gifts of untold worth and antiquity. He will lie about eating rich, fattening foods and testing the quality of all the wines in the kingdom.

It is important here to note that the Libra/Pig perceives everything through a haze of his above-described secret dream world, and because of this is truly handicapped when it comes to dealing with bland drudgery. He can go through the motions of routine and seem surprisingly efficient at dull tasks. But Libra/Pig is not really there. He or she is waiting for the next moment of romantic exaltation to occur. The dishes and the floor-scrubbing will get done. But Libra/Pig's soul is elsewhere.

Many of the Libra/Pig's dreams never come true. He or she will not really be an effective world-beating type. The word "talented" comes to mind. Libra/Pig is very adept at creative pursuits. But the rocky road to realization of projects often discourages the fragile soul of the artistic Libra/Pig before he accomplishes the project. His or her mind may overshoot the goal, leap ahead of the finishing line, and the project, of course, bogs down en route.

What arises, then, is anger, bitterness and quarrelsomeness. When too many dreams are dashed, when too many hopes have been scrapped, resentment builds up. Many Libra/Pigs die resenting the whole human race for its inability to comprehend what they were getting at in the first place.

The best thing Libra/Pigs can do is settle down with someone who adores them for their pacific tastes and ability to add grace to any hovel. The Libra/Pig's strongest suits are his charm, his capacity for blind, tireless love and his sensuality. If he insists on ruling, then he ought to do so from the wings of a safe and pleasant house in the country whence he does not often venture into the fracas of metropolitan life. Libra/Pig needs equilibrium and reacts badly to all outside resistance to his whims.

Love

At the risk of redundancy, I remark here that the Libra/Pig's best shot is in the love department. He is able to give of himself in personal interchange and shared complicity better than most other human beings. Libra/Pig is self-sacrificial where his or her mate is concerned. The pleasure of Libra/Pig's life is mostly derived vicariously through the achievements of those he loves. As for himself? Well, he can't really decide what his preferences are. He probably doesn't want much more than love, comfort and a few stabs at an artistic hobby or two.

If you love one of these people, you already know that they are willing (although sometimes a tad resistant at first) to give up everything of their own for the sake of your happiness and advancement. What you must give in return is, however, no mean compensation. Libra/Pig wants luxury, comfort, and utter and complete devotion. Don't fail him. You'll pay dearly.

Compatibilities

Your romantic leanings predispose you to getting on with Cats and Goats. You appreciate their discretion. Try to commit yourself to a Gemini, Sagittarius, Leo or Aquarius/Cat or Goat lover. Snakes in general are proscribed for Pigs, and your worst choices would come from Aries, Cancer or Capricorn-born Serpents. You don't get along with Capricorn/Monkeys, either. Too cerebral and not funky enough for your sensual streak. Dragons? Maybe. A sweetie-pie Cancer or a noble-spirited Capricorn/Dragon could enhance your existence.

Home and Family

The home of a Libra/Pig will be a showplace of comfortable luxury. One thing these people know how to do is contribute beauty to any environment in which they live. They will always prefer the ornate to the practical, the majestic to the humble. A lot of the time, their tastes are expensively out-of-reach which doesn't help in the bitterness department.

Libra/Pig parents may have a tendency to feel that children only run a close second to their mates. They are dutiful toward their offspring. But they often give more attention and affection to their partners. Still, children round out the happy picture for Libra/Pigs and so they are essential to their well-being. The children of these sweet, giving people can ask almost any service of their Libra/Pig parent. It's impossible for Libra/Pigs to say "no," especially to a dish of ice cream or an extra helping of dessert.

Profession

The Libra/Pig native is always interested in social advancement. But again, this progress translates best only insofar as it applies to the union in which the Libra/Pig is involved. Love first. Achievement later. Social betterment only within the realm of the couple. The Libra/Pig is mightily talented and certainly adept at all manner of undertaking. But he won't go it alone. Libra/Pig will get involved professionally if said career improves the lot of the alliance that he or she has chosen as lifestyle.

This person makes a hesitant boss. As he is not attracted to domination or interested in taking charge of others, he finds supervising painful and nerve-wracking. The Libra/Pig would probably rather be bossed than be a boss. As an employee he is responsible and industrious so long as his romantic life is functioning smoothly. If he or she has a row with hubby or wife, the day will surely be ruined and a black cloud of uncertainty will hang over the Libra/Pig's head. For Librans born in Pig years everything that matters involves what belongs to him or her, what he or she cares for and loves. The rest is gingerbread.

Libra/Pigs excel at everything having to do with the home. They make good homemakers, wonderful farmers and chefs, restaurateurs and wine growers.

Some famous Libra/Pigs: Le Corbusier, Julie Andrews, Cheryl Tiegs, Chris Kirkpatrick, Emmanuelle Laborit, France Gall, Jenna Elfman, Jacques Manière, Julien Clerc, Kevin Richardson, Luciano Pavarotti, Melina Mercouri, Michel Oliver, Vaughn Monroe.

Other books by Suzanne White

CHINESE ASTROLOGY PLAIN AND SIMPLE
THE NEW ASTROLOGY
LA DOUBLE ASTROLOGIE
LA DOBLE ASTROLOGIA
THE NEW CHINESE ASTROLOGY
LA NEUVA ASTROLOGIA CHINA
THE ASTROLOGY OF LOVE
LADYFINGERS (A NOVEL)
BALD IN THE MERDE (A NOVELETTE)

Available in all formats (ebook and paper) from all Booksellers

Personal Telephone Readings, Books, Chapters, Horoscopes and Lifestyle Advice at http://www.suzannewhite.com

Printed in Great Britain
by Amazon